Visualizat

2 Books in 1: Visualization and Visualization Techniques!

2 Books in 1

BOX SET

Book # 1: Visualization Techniques

Contents

Book # 2: Visualization

Contents

Book # 1

Visualization Techniques

The Best Creative Visualization Techniques to Unlock Your Hidden Potential Using Meditation and Your Imagination

---

Copyright © 2015

Neither the author nor the publisher assumes any responsibility or liability whatsoever on the behalf of the purchaser or reader of these materials.

Any received slight of any individual or organization is purely unintentional.

Introduction

I want to thank you and congratulate you for downloading the book, "Creative Visualization: The Best Visualization Techniques to Unlock Your Hidden Potential Using Meditation and Your Imagination".

This book contains proven steps and strategies on how to etch out the path of success using meditation and your imagination.

Creative visualization is nothing but a mental technique guided by imagination to make your goals and dreams come true. When used in the right way, creative visualization can boost your life and take you through to the stairs of success and prosperity. It is like a power that brings certain changes to your environment, the circumstances and influences the occurrence of certain events. Creative visualization can bring money, love, possessions, work and people into your life. It uses the power of your mind and frankly speaking, this the only power involved behind every successful man.

Thanks again for downloading this book, I hope you enjoy it!

Chapter 1: What is Creative Visualization?

Creative visualization is nothing but a mental technique guided by imagination to make your goals and dreams come true. When used in the right way, creative visualization can boost your life and take you through to the stairs of success and prosperity. It is like a power that brings certain changes to your environment, the circumstances and influences the occurrence of certain events. Creative visualization can bring money, love, possessions, work and people into your life. It uses the power of your mind and frankly speaking, this the only power involved behind every successful man.

If you visualize a certain event or a particular situation, you can always attract into your life. This is much like daydreaming to be frank, but the effects can simply be magical. Although it is guided by the natural ability of your mind or mental laws, but it is very much like a genie in your fingertips.

Many people use creative visualization in their day-day affairs knowingly or unknowingly. All successful people use it not realizing it as a proven source of power. They simply focus on their goals and see them as already accomplished. Their focus and perseverance in this creative visualization actually brings in the success that they want in life.

Chapter 2: How and why does Creative Visualization work?

Our mind can essentially be divided in two parts; the conscious mind and the sub-conscious mind. The sub-conscious mind imbibes the thoughts that keep repeating all throughout the day. When it imbibes these thoughts, it alters your mindset also along with your habits day-day activities. This brings you closer to certain people, circumstances or situations.

Thoughts are often guided by a creative mind that sets the tone for your life, thereby attracting things you want to achieve in life. Thoughts get absorbed from one mind to another and can be picked up by people unconsciously. So, you never know when you come in contact with a person who can actually help you fulfill your goals and desires.

We are very much a part of the Omnipotent power, the one that has made this universe. So, we constantly take part in the process of creation. Therefore, there is absolutely no wonder why thoughts continuously seep into our minds. Being so closely associated with this universal power, it is quite likely that our thoughts will come true. But, do all our dreams come true?

No. It is the dream that is focused, well-nourished and keeps repeating all through the day. Thought process (especially a focused thought) is a form of energy as it is filled with emotions. Thoughts alter the balance of our surroundings and bring the changes to the environment accordingly.

Many people repeatedly think about certain things. The thoughts are mainly based on the current situation or circumstances. So, these produce and reproduce the same kind of situations or circumstances. It is very much like watching the same film again and again. But, you can change the film by altering your thoughts and your attitude over things.

Chapter 3: Simple steps to practice Creative Visualization effectively

In order to practice creative visualization, one does not need to be a believer of any spiritual or metaphysical ideas. You have to be open to certain concepts even if you don't believe in e supernatural power. You need to have the desire of enriching your knowledge, your experience and be open to new ideas and concepts.

Simple steps for practicing effective creative visualization

Getting the timing right: Creative visualization is best when done in a relaxed and positive frame of mind. It is good if you take a long hot water bath at night, listen to some relaxing music on your earphones and indulge yourself in meditation for a couple of minutes. Although it is very hard to do this in today's fast paced life, but you can at least meditate for 5 minutes (at night), before visualizing even if you do not get time for other things.

Decide on your goal: Pick out something that you wish to have, create, realize or work for in life. It can be a job, an apartment, relationship, improved mental or physical health or a peaceful state of mind. First, you should always set yourself with simple goals that you wish to fulfill in your near future. This will not cause too much negative resistance in the first place as you will be able to taste success as you are mastering creative visualization techniques. Once you master a different set of techniques and gather the much needed experience, you can try taking more critical issues or challenges.

Visualize or create a clear picture of your goals: Once you start to feel relaxed and positive, gently close your eyes and try to visualize a mental picture of the object or the condition you want to achieve. Always think of it in present tense and consider it to be existent exactly the same way you want it to be. Put yourself in the situation and add as many details you want.

Many people often feel difficulties in visualizing this step. So, let us assume the following scenario to make it a little easier for you. Suppose, you wish to go for a vacation on a beach; you can start off by getting the feel, trying to realize the warmness and the light breeze swaying all over the beach. Then focus on the sounds. Try to feel the seagulls roaring, the waves, the people talking and the kids playing around. After you feel the sounds, focus on the scenic elements such as people walking, swimming or surfing on the beach, children making sand castles, the blue skies, the sunny morning etc. Now put yourself in the situation and try to feel all the aspects together. Although visualizing for 5 minutes or so, rarely has the much desired impact, but you will get to know how creative visualization is actually done.

Focus on your goals quite often: Bring your idea or the mental picture in your mind quite often, both during quiet meditation periods and repeatedly throughout the day. This way, it will be an integral part of your life and much like a reality.

Focus on it precisely in a gentle and relaxed manner. Do not strive too hard and put excessive stress on yourself. This will tend to hamper things rather than being helpful. Creative visualization is useless if you do it once in a few days. Try doing it at least once every day. Though it is okay if you skip one day after a few weeks for some reason, you should always focus on the goal constantly before it actually materializes.

Having the positive vibe within you is very important. When you focus on your goal, always think of it in a positive frame of mind. Strongly believe and repeat to yourself that it already exists. Dream that you will achieve or receive it in the very next moment. Such positive thoughts are usually referred to as affirmations. While having such affirmative thoughts, you should never be in a state of doubt or disbelief. Try to think that your goals are already accomplished and very much existent in reality.

Continue with the same technique until your goal is actually accomplished or you do not have the desire of carrying it any further. Goals can always change before they actually materialize and this is completely natural considering the growth and development of any human being. So, never try to stick to a goal if you do not have the energy or desire for it. When you lose interest in something, it is time for you to look for a new point of interest.

When your goal changes, always try to acknowledge the change and then nourish the fresh set of goals. Be absolutely sure that you are no longer targeting the previous goal. In such cases, you should discard the old and try to imbibe the new one as early as you can. This will negate any sort of confusion or failure as you know that your goals have changed.

Once the goal is achieved, always try to acknowledge your success We often achieve things as per our want or desire but forget to notice and acknowledge the success. So, appreciate the fact that you have succeeded and give yourself a pat on the back. Finally, you should thank the almighty and the universe for giving you the opportunity of fulfilling your goals.

6. How much time does it take: Well, it usually depends how big your goal actually is. In case of a smaller goal, it can simply take a few days. If you want a girlfriend, it can just take you 1 or 2 weeks. But if you have bigger goals like buying an apartment, getting a promotion in the office, it can certainly take a few months. There is no determining factor of the time required. Bigger goals will obviously take a bit more time as compared to smaller ones.

Some Do's and Don'ts for you to remember

• Even if you do not see any change after practicing creative visualization, do not stop the process and express doubts about it. If you stop thinking it will not happen, you are actually expressing doubts over the universal power. Stopping the practice will simply allow your desires to die much like an un-watered plant.

• Don't give up the practice if the results do not show in a few days, weeks or months. Continue following all the steps sincerely and results will certainly show up at some point of time.

• When you have strong doubts about this technique, you should first drive these doubts out of your mind. Doubts will certainly hinder your act of creative visualization, thereby preventing the results to come. Start off with small and simple goals in the beginning and once they get fulfilled, your belief in creative visualization will grow much stronger.

• Read the success stories from different celebrities. Do not discuss this technique with your friends and relatives, if they are not too open-minded (i.e. not willing to accept new ideas). Their doubts may oppose your belief and increase your doubts even further.

• Try to practice creative visualization every night at least for 10-20 minutes in a relaxed and positive frame of mind.

• Watch the movie "The Secret" to get a clear idea about creative visualization. Read other articles on the internet about creative visualization if you want to practice this act sincerely.

A Few Things which you should keep in mind

• Do not believe that this is not for real. It certainly works for all. Read the success stories of celebrities, who used to follow creative visualization and achieved what they wanted in life.

• Do not think that the results will come if you do nothing and wait for some magic to happen. You will have to take inspiration from people who have succeeded and act sincerely towards fulfilling your goal. Your thoughts and inspired action will certainly influence the universe to change the course of events, the people and circumstances around you to take you closer to your goals.

• You can never reach your goal if you consider it to be impossible. Always believe that it is possible and work yourself towards it. The results will automatically follow.

Chapter 4: Effects of Creative Visualization

Creative Visualization catalyzes the process of healing

Creative visualization is often used by athletes to boost their performance. A golfer is known to visualize in their mind a perfect swing on numerous occasions. This will mentally charge the muscle memory.

Now let us look at a well known study about the effect of creative visualization on sports.

A bunch of Olympic athletes was divided into 3 different groups. Group 1 was offered 100% physical training. The athletes in Group 2 received 75% physical training and 25% mental conditioning. Group 3 athletes on the other had received 50% of physical training and 50 % of mental conditioning. It was seen that the athletes in Group 3 scored highest in terms of performance. So, this helps us conclude that mental images act as a trigger to muscular impulses (a widely accepted or understood principle in sports psychology or neuroscience).

Creative Visualization catalyzes the process of healing

We have come across plenty of success stories about creative visualization boosting the process of healing. People are known to report to have healed themselves (from cancer) and many other ailments owing to creative visualization. A man in his eighties actually visualized blood sprouting from his veins, and some birds feeding on the toxins coming out of the unhealthy cells. To be honest, you have to believe that you can and the rest will eventually take its course.

Chapter 5: Success stories from various celebrities

Many celebrities are known to have reaped the benefits of creative visualization. Some of them are Oprah Winfrey, Bill Gates, Tiger Woods, Arnold Schwarzenegger, Will Smith, Jim Carrey, Anthony Robbins and Drew Barrymore. There is significant evidence that even Winston Churchill and William Shakespeare used creative visualization to etch out their success. Many have used creative visualization to get over their challenges and saw their success much before they actually became successful.

Jim Carrey actually wrote a 10 million $ check for himself in the year 1987. He dated the check for Thanksgiving Day, year 1995 and quoted "for acting services rendered" on top of the check. He focused on it for years until he finally received a sum of 10 million $ for his performance in Dumb and Dumber.

During an interview in the year 2007, Oprah Winfrey told the talk show host that one can really change his or her reality based on the way he or she thinks.

Arnold Schwarzenegger believes that it is all in our minds. He has labeled the mind as an incredible asset. Before he won the first Mr. Universe title, he actually walked around the tournament visualizing that he was already the winner. He believed that the title belonged to him, till he finally won it. He claims to have done the same thing in his acting career. He visualized himself of being a successful actor, earning lots of money.

Justin Timberlake says that people can even move things with their minds if they are really focused.

Elvis Presley, the legendary rock star says that he was a dreamer in his childhood days. He read comic books and considered himself to be the hero of the story. When he saw a movie, he considered himself as the hero of the movie. He says that every dream that he dreamt has proved to be real time and again.

Ace basketball player Michael Jordan says he always visualized what he wanted to be in life, what kind of player he actually wanted to be. He always knew where he wanted to reach and always visualized getting there.

Chapter 6: Illustration of Creative Visualization by Wallace Wattles

Wallace Wattles described the concept of visualization in his bestselling book "The Science of Getting Rich (1910)". Every individual having an interest about the power of mind is aware about him or has read this book. "The Science of Getting Rich (1910)" has had phenomenal success and is still one of the most widely studied books till date. This book still holds the same kind of popularity as it used to bear 100 years back.

In "The Science of Getting Rich (1910)", the author shares his thoughts or insights on being rich or getting anything as per your want or desire. Wattles conceptualized creative visualization and literally carried a movement on this thought process. He inspired many authors, including Napoleon Hill. The book and the movie "The Secret" was primarily based on his insights about creative visualization.

According to Wallace Wattles, every aspect of our life ah emerged from thoughts. The universe is guided by the thought process and whatever we think in our life, it actually becomes bigger and materialistic in real life.

Wallace says in his book that if we think that we live in a new house, dress up in fine clothes, drive a car for our day to day journey, we can be confident about everything. He advises to imagine an environment or a monetary stability as you have always wanted and then live each of these imaginary situations time and again. This, according to him will actually bring the change we actually look for in our lives.

Wattles remarked that if an individual can reciprocate his thoughts to an existing thought process or belief, he can influence the formation or creation of the substance he focuses on.

According to him, one should always stay focused about his goal or objectives till it is actually achieved. He or she should think about it continuously and accept it as the hard reality. When you have decided about the goal, begin to think that it is already yours or on the way. Think of it again and again so that the universe also takes it as your reality.

Be clear about your goal or desire a repeatedly think about it in your mind. Do not think about the present situations or circumstances as these might hinder your steps towards success.

Wallace Wattles says that one should be grateful for whatever he or she has got. Gratitude connects you with the power. People may give it the name of God, the Spirit or the Divine. This energy or connection is actually the one which facilitates the change or manifestation of visualization. Gratitude opens up the vibration points of your system and subjects you to a state of acceptance or open-mindedness.

Wallace Wattles says that there are many things that combine to make you successful in life. So, you should be grateful for all the things that actually contributed towards your success.

Chapter 7: Eliminating Limited Thinking

Creative visualization can certainly help you achieve great things in life. But in some persons, there are certain areas that cannot be changed too easily or at least in the near future. Creative visualization is immensely powerful, but there are some limitations. These limitations exist within us, and not in the power.

We often restrict ourselves and fail to look beyond a certain radius. We confine ourselves to the thoughts and ideologies and restrict ourselves to the life we actually live.

One needs to be open minded and set bigger targets. This will put us closer to bigger opportunities or possibilities. Limitations are within our minds and it is our responsibility to bring the change. The change may take some time to materialize. Small and short- term changes may occur in quick time but bigger transformations will certainly take a bit longer.

You need to have faith and keep trying. The results will start to appear automatically.

Conclusion

Thank you again for downloading this book!

I hope this book was able to help you to reach your goals using creative visualization and the power of your imagination.

The next step is to suggest this book to your friends and relatives, if you feel it will benefit them too. Always remember that creative visualization is immensely powerful, but there are some limitations to its success. These limitations exist within us, and not in the power.

Finally, if you enjoyed this book, please take the time to share your thoughts and post a review on Amazon. It'd be greatly appreciated!

Thank you and good luck!

Book # 2

Visualization

The Most Effective Creative Visualization
Techniques to Achieve Success Using Meditation,
Imagination and Brain Training

Introduction

I want to thank you and congratulate you for downloading the book, "Visualization Techniques: The Most Effective Creative Visualization Techniques to Achieve Success Using Meditation, Imagination and Brain Training."

This book contains proven steps and strategies on how to use creative visualization to reach all of your life goals.

If you follow the steps that are set forth in this book you will soon open your mind to new experiences, positive energy that make all of your wishes come true with just a few simple exercises.

Thanks again for downloading this book, I hope you enjoy it!

Chapter 1: What is Creative Visualization?

Everyone has goals in life that wanted to be reached. Whether you are an athlete wishing to perform better, an artist trying to be more creative, anyone who is trying to improve his career and looking for different ways to succeed. Creative visualization is a tool that you can use to help yourself open your mind up completely and easily reach every goal that you want to.

The skill of creative visualization engages the right side of your brain and activates your prefrontal cortex. It helps to increase your creative skills and lets you think of things in a different way. This means that you can find alternative options that may have been hiding right under your nose the whole time. In a way, it's a wonderful type of a catch 22. As you grow your imagination skills, you will become even better at visualization and, in turn as you work on your visualization skills you will soon see that you have more imaginative thoughts. It all works in combination to make your mind stronger!

This is skill that everyone can learn to utilize while using meditation techniques and your imagination in order to expand your mind and fully achieve the things in life that might seem difficult or even impossible. You can use creative visualization techniques without learning meditation, however when including all facets of these brain training methods, you will easily reach the pinnacle of mastery much quicker and with a higher success rate. In addition, as you get better at creative visualization your imagination will grow stronger as well, which can lead to better problem solving skills on a daily basis for you.

This book will teach you all of the skills that you need to be able to meditate properly and to convert that action into better creative visualization techniques. It will also explain some helpful imagination building tools and some great ways to train your brain to become more attuned to the world around you and the metaphysical world that might seem just out of your reach. You will soon be well on your way to making all of your dreams come true!

Chapter 2: Meditation Skills To Help With Visualization

One of the first things to focus on when you first start looking into the process of creative visualization techniques is different types of meditation. If you have never explored any type of meditation techniques then it may seem like a confusing process. In addition, you may not realize that there are actually several different methods that you can try in order to find the one that suits you personally. Your mind is just as unique as the rest of you, so it's important that you explore all of your options and then make the choice that fits you just right. Let's look at a couple of different meditation techniques to start you on your path to self-discovery.

Steps to Basic Meditation

- *Get Ready*

  Ensure that you have a comfortable space for meditation. You might have trouble achieving a trance where you sleep at and experts also add that you will be most successful in a seated position. But, it's a personal process so it comes down to where you are most likely able to alter your state of being. You should turn the lights down or off and ensure that you are totally comfortable in whatever area you pick.

- *Get Comfortable*

  Remove your shoes and make sure that you're not wearing tight fitting clothing so that you don't constrict your movement. When you start trying to concentrate your thoughts, uncomfortable clothes can be the only focus that you can find! You should ensure that you're not hungry and that you didn't just eat a big meal to prevent other distractions. When you get more practice you'll be able to meditate no matter what is going on around you, but in the beginning you will want try to make it an easier process.

- **Remove Distractions**

  In order to rid your mind of distractions and focus your thoughts you need to eliminate as many distracting influences as you can. Turn off your phone so you don't have any interruptions. If you want to use a c.d. or other aid for meditation, ensure that it's set up; but you don't need these to achieve your goals in meditation. Plus, thiscan actually lessen your abilities, because you will easily get too used to them and won't be able to enter a trance as easily without them in the background.

- **Be Relaxed**

  Sit up tall and straighten your spine; you can picture the top of your head pulling your back straight up and down. With your eyes closed, start relaxing every part of your body, one piece at a time. Begin at your feet and move up, focusing on every muscle and joint. Continue moving up your whole body and don't forget your head and face.

- **Breathe**

  Sit in your relaxed state of being and focus only on breathing. Just concentrate on the way it feels when you inhale the air into your lungs and when you exhale it back out through your mouth.

- **Have a Mantra**

  If you recite a simple mantra along with your breaths it can help you improve your focus. This mantra can be as simple "breathe in, breathe out". It's only important to ensure that you don't concentrate too much on what you are saying; the words are just to improve your concentration on clearing your mind.

- ***Empty Your Thoughts***
  When you're focusing only on the mantra and your breath, you will empty thoughts from your head. Don't worry if it takes you a bit to get into the swing of things, this will take you some practice.

- ***Finishing Up***
  If you're finished meditating and ready to come back to the physical world, slowly count down from five while you keep your eyes closed. Come back to physical awareness in a slow manner and open your eyes. Try building up your meditation skills with short sessions to make sure you are getting quality over quantity. You should consider starting with 5 minute sessions two times a day, and add more from there.

In addition to this one main method of meditation, there are also several other ways to get into the state of mind that you are aiming for, so let's look at some alternatives.

Focus on Breathing

The first method to look at is simply just leaning to focus on your breathing to transport yourself into a meditative state. This is one of the most basic methods that we are going to look at.

- Find a comfortable sitting position on the floor, a chair or a cushion in a quiet, peaceful location.

- Close your eyes and press your tongue gently up to your palate. With your mouth closed, breathe only through your nose.
- Inhale deeply through your nose, and let the air fill your abdomen. Next, exhale completely through your slightly opened mouth. Focus only on your breathing as you continue to breathe in and out.
- Don't think about your breathing, just focus to clear your mind completely.

Walking Meditation

It sounds counterproductive; however you can also meditate while walking. With this method of meditation your focus is on your feet as opposed to your breathing.

- As you walk, simply focus on the act of your step on the ground.
- Don't allow your eyes or your mind to wander away from your focus.
- Keep your eyes in front of you and continue focusing on each step as you move forward.

There is entire host of different ways for you to enter a meditative state. These three are just beginning options and if they work well for you then, you can either stick with them or find some new ones to explore. Meditation is really just the beginning when it comes to opening up your awareness and learning how to engage in the art of creative visualization. Remember, don't worry if you have trouble meditating at first, it will take some time to get used to your new practice and find the true enjoyment in it. Just keep working on it, so that you can get closer to reaching you ultimate goal of using creative visualization to reach all of you goals in life.

Chapter 3: Exercises to Build Your Imagination

On top of your new meditation skills, you will want to work on building up your imagination. When you were a child, you could do anything or build anything in your mind, but growing up kills that feature in so many people. Imagination is an integral part of achieving success using creative visualization. Now is the time for you to recapture that lost imagination and learn to harness its power, so let's look at some exercises that can help build it back up for you.

Take up some new activities.

Try doing some different things in your daily life. Take day trips to new places around you, pick up some new hobbies or even just read a different kind of book then you usually do. It's important to notice new things and have some fresh experiences to help break you out of your habits. This is a fairly easy thing to start with, but you will have to remind yourself that you are trying to make room for new things in your life and move outside your normal, comfortable realm.

Find joy in the simple things.

Children don't need complicated things to make their lives more playful or enjoyable. Try taking a day to yourself and just looking at things from the perspective of a child. Go out and play, and don't worry about how anyone looks at you. Think about how a child can go from drawing a picture to pretending that they are a monkey to making something out of what just looked like old trash. They find simple things to amuse themselves with and turn them into whatever they want them to be. You can do this, too. While you may feel silly and out of place at first, that's exactly what you are going for, so revel in it.

Play some games.

Start incorporating some new games into your day. Find some nice puzzle games or try the type that require you to think things through or use more creative reasoning to accomplish the tasks required of you. These can help you expand your imagination by thinking in different ways than you are used to.

Start keeping a journal.

As you try to expand your horizons and alter your reality, you should start keeping a journal for yourself. Write all of your creative thoughts down. You can even use it for drawings or things that you find that give you a little spark. It will help you focus your energy in more imaginative ways.

Start paying attention to everything.

Take a moment to really look at things. No matter what you are doing during the day, think about how things actually look, how things feel and everything else about them. Look at your surroundings and examine things in more detail. Pay attention to the way the wind really feels, the true colors in everything and all of the textures that you feel. This is an important exercise because when you start trying to visualize you will be much more successful when you picture them in a greater detail and truly feel the things that you are aiming for.

Start practicing some training techniques.

There are actually a huge amount of exercises out there that are specifically designed to train your mind to regain some of the imagination that you once reveled in as a child. These usually only take a small amount of time out of your busy day, however they can be well worth that time in what they can do for you. Here are a few methods for you to try out.

Paying Attention to Details

Start with some paper and a pencil and a magazine. Pick a page at random and look at the picture. After 1 minute passes, close the magazine and start writing. Make a list of everything that you can remember from the picture and when you finish, go back and look it over again to see if there is anything else you could have added or anything that you got wrong. You can practice this exercise several times a day with just a little free time and it won't take long for you to notice that you are seeing more things for your list each time that you do it.

Change Your Perspective

You really want to start changing the way that you think about your reality and stretch your imagination to its furthest limits. Take some time out each day and make yourself think outside the box. Think about how things would be if you were an animal. Don't just think on the surface, but actually concentrate on the details of the situation. Picture yourself in situations that you could never be in, like at the bottom of the deepest sea, or floating through space without a suit. When you try to see things from other perspectives, make sure that you are actually building the world around you. This is a little bit like the creative visualization that we will be getting further in depth with, but it's more just a fun little past time to keep building on your imagination.

Everything included in this chapter is there to help you adjust the way that you think and make your imagination strong again. Between meditation and teaching your brain to see things in a different light, you will be ready to envision everything that you want to and achieve all of the success you long for in life. Using these tools will set you up in the proper way to be able to use creative visualization and make sure it's a pleasant, fun and successful endeavor for you.

Chapter 4: Using Creative Visualization to Win

You have learned some great ways to build your imagination and some easy techniques to help with your meditation skills, but now you are probably getting anxious to learn some actual methods to use creative visualization to reach for your waiting success. Now we can go over a simple way to tie all of this together and really make it work wonders for you.

Relax and Prepare

Make sure that you are in the right frame of mind when you first sit down to start visualizing the way that you want things to go. Create an environment that fosters relaxation and puts you in a positive state. Set your preferred area up for your meditation and get very comfortable with it. Try to meditate for at least 5-10 minutes, or longer if that's what you want. It's just important to make sure that you are focused, relaxed and positive.

Visualize

Once you are in the right state of mind, start your visualizations. Make sure you see yourself in the situation that you are aiming for in very specific detail. Imagine everything from the sights and smells to the feelings that you will experience when it happens. Really take the time to sense all of the pieces of your vision and all of the ways that it will go right. Don't focus on anything negative; instead make sure that you are fully committed to the positive outcome that will happen. Strong, positive energy is what will make you successful and you have to work for those feelings and not allow the negativity to seep in.

Don't Stop

Creative visualization isn't something that will work if you just do it once in a while. Try to make it a part of your everyday routine. You have to keep the positive thoughts flowing and this can only happen when you surround yourself with it all of the time. Don't give up if it seems to take longer than you expected, just keep going and continue to visualize your goals.

Visualize During the Day

Not only should you be thinking about your goals while actively participating in a creative visualization session, but also at other times as well. You should picture you reaching your success as you go about your daily routines and make sure that you believe that these things can truly happen for you. By having this confidence and expecting the good things to happen to you, they will eventually happen. Again, not everything that you are trying to make happen will come to pass overnight, however you can make them happen sooner by completely wrapping yourself in the belief that they will.

Chapter 5: Visualizing During the Day

It's important to keep in mind that you are in control of manifesting the positive changes in your life. One recent study involving several groups of athletes showed that the group that supplemented their usual practice with the same amount of time spent on visualization performed better than groups that included only a little or no time spent visualizing. These results should help show you that you can certainly reach your goals as well by using these same techniques. When you are reminding yourself of your goals during the day, there are a few things that can also help you.

Tell Yourself

Put the thoughts of your success at the forefront of your mind as often as possible. When you shower in the morning, spend your time daydreaming about them. When you are getting ready in front of the mirror, say them out loud. When you are in the car, speak them out loud again. Make these visualizations a part of everything that you do every day.

Write Them Down

For many people, the written word is a very powerful thing. Write down exactly what you are hoping to gain and look over it whenever you feel like it is getting away from. Keep expanding on it in your journal and enjoy your elaborations on it. This can also help with your actual times of dedicated creative visualizations by giving you more focus to think about.

Make a Board

When you see an image or text that strongly reminds you of the goals that you are striving for, you should save it. Make a physical vision board collecting all of these things in order to help focus your energy. If you can see what you are aiming for it can help you work even harder to reach your goals. This makes a complete visual picture for you to focus on and to feel even more like your dreams are well within your grasp. By doing this, you are also giving yourself a constant reminder to remain positive and to keep your mind open to new opportunities that you might have otherwise missed.

Chapter 6: Other Things to Remember

Creative visualization is about changing your perception of the world around you and allowing positive energy to find you. It assists in programming your mind to be accepting of the success that you are looking for and to open your mind to new opportunities that can take you where you want to go.

Don't give up, even if it seems to be taking a long time for you to be getting where you want to be. Just keep practicing your skills and soon everything will open up for you.

When you combine the strength of your imagination, your new meditation skills and all of the positive energy held within you then you can easily manifest the things in your life that you deserve. Enjoy your new life!

Conclusion

Thank you again for downloading this book!

I hope this book was able to help you to reach your goals to achieve success using creative visualization.

The next step is to suggest this book to your friends and relatives, if you feel it will benefit them too. Remember that you can get everything that you want out of your life and the mediation, imagination and training exercises in this book can take you a long way!

Finally, if you enjoyed this book, please take the time to share your thoughts and post a review on Amazon. It'd be greatly appreciated!

Thank you and good luck!

10999863R00027

Printed in Great Britain
by Amazon.co.uk, Ltd.,
Marston Gate.